D0567936

THE WAR IN AFGHANISTAN

BY JENNIFER ZEIGER

CHILDREN'S PRESS®

An Imprint of Scholastic Inc.

New York Toronto London Auckland Sydney
Mexico City New Delhi Hong Kong
Danbury, Connecticut

Content Consultant
Christopher Gelpi, PhD
Professor of Political Science
Duke University
Durham, North Carolina

Library of Congress Cataloging-in-Publication Data

Zeiger, Jennifer.
  The War in Afghanistan / Jennifer Zeiger.
      p. cm. —(Cornerstones of freedom)
  Includes bibliographical references and index.
  ISBN-13: 978-0-531-25044-0 (lib. bdg.)   ISBN-10: 0-531-25044-X (lib. bdg.)
  ISBN-13: 978-0-531-26569-7 (pbk.)   ISBN-10: 0-531-26569-2 (pbk.)
  1. Afghan War, 2001—Juvenile literature. 2. Afghanistan—
History—2001—Juvenile literature. I. Title. II. Series.
  DS371.412.Z45 2011
  958.104'7—dc22   2011009488

1 2 3 4 5 6 7 8 9 10 R 21 20 19 18 17 16 15 14 13 12

Photographs © 2012: Alamy Images: 24 (Scott J. Ferrell/Congressional
Quarterly), 53 top (Harald Lüder/F1online digitale Bildagentur GmbH);
AP Images: 42 (Rodrigo Abd), 22, 58 bottom (Frank Augstein), 52 (Adam
Butler), 38 (Victor Ruiz Caballero), 5 left, 15 (K.M. Choudary), 34 (Dima
Gavrysh), 44, 57 (Julie Jacobson), 39 (Noor Khan), 12 (Dimitri Messinis), 30
(Emilio Morenatti), 53 bottom (Anjum Naveed), 43 (PRNewsFoto/The Asia
Foundation), 50, 51 (Musadeq Sadeq), 5 right, 8 (Murad Sezer), 37 (Amir
Shah), 31, 32, 33, 56 bottom, 59 (Manish Swarup), 4 bottom, 28 (Richard
Vogel), 14 (Apichart Weerawong), 7; Getty Images: 11 (Vitaly Armand/AFP),
54 (Adek Berry/AFP), 21 (Romeo Gacad/AFP), 16, 56 top (Greg Mathieson/
Mai/Time Life Pictures), 41 (John Moore), 26 (Robert Nickelsberg), 10,
58 top (Robert Nickelsberg/Time Life Pictures), 18 (Paul J. Richards/
AFP), 4 top, 6 (David Stewart-Smith); Jennifer Zeiger: 64; Landov, LLC: 27
(Luke Frazza/Reuters), 23 (Reuters/STR), 46 (Pete Souza/EPA); Reuters: 36
(Roberto Escobar), back cover (Finbarr O'Reilly), cover (Bob Strong); U.S.
Army Photo/Staff Sgt. Ryan C. Matson: 2, 3, 48; U.S. Navy Photo: 20 (Chief
Photographer's Mate Johnny Bivera/Fleet Combat Camera Atlantic), 40
(Mass Communication Specialist 2nd Class Jason Johnston).

Did you know that studying history can be fun?

BRING HISTORY TO LIFE by becoming a history investigator. Examine the evidence (primary and secondary source materials); cross-examine the people and witnesses. Take a look at what was happening at the time—but be careful! What happened years ago might suddenly become incredibly interesting and change the way you think!

Contents

Unrest in Afghanistan

The mujahideen spent many years fighting for control of Afghanistan.

After years of discontent, civil war broke out in Afghanistan during the 1970s. What became known as the Afghan War began in 1978, when the existing Afghan government was forced out. A new one was set up in its place. Many Afghans did not support the new government and fought against it. These fighters became known as the **mujahideen**, or "holy warriors." They believed that they were fighting on the side of God and Islam against an immoral government.

One year later, the Soviet Union sent about 30,000 soldiers into Afghanistan. They toppled the existing government and allowed a different group to take control. This made other foreign nations nervous. To keep the Soviet Union from taking power, Pakistan, Saudi Arabia, and the United States helped the mujahideen. They sent money and weapons and helped train soldiers. With this aid, the mujahideen were able to defeat the Soviets. By 1989, no Soviet troops remained in Afghanistan, but this victory did not end Afghanistan's civil war. Thousands died as **ethnic** groups and political parties continued to compete for power.

New weapons helped the mujahideen defeat the Soviets.

KILLED IN THE AFGHAN WAR.

CHAPTER 1

THE TALIBAN

Years of conflict have caused damage to many buildings in Afghanistan.

The mujahideen finally

took control of the Afghan government in 1992. The former president was forced out of power, and the victorious mujahideen set up a new government.

Fighting within the government and rebellion from outside it soon caused the new government to collapse. Mujahideen groups that had once been allies now fought each other for power. New rebel groups sprang up and placed their own claims on the government.

Members of the Taliban follow a very strict form of Islam.

Continued Conflict

Each group had its own ethnic ties and political ideas.
A shared ethnicity meant a shared culture and history.
Political ideas defined how these groups believed the
government should be run. Each group fought to stake
its own claim on the capital city of Kabul.

Groups were also motivated by religion. Most
Afghans are Muslim. They follow Islam, a religion based
on the teachings of the Prophet Muhammad. Much of
the nation's population felt that Islam should be part
of the government. However, like all religions, Islam's
teachings can be understood in many different ways. Not
all rebel groups interpreted the religion the same way.

Rebels from the South

One rebel group with especially extreme beliefs was the Taliban. *Taliban* means "students." Its members were students from the Kandahar region in southern Afghanistan. They had been students in U.S.- and Pakistan-supported schools in the refugee camps that had been set up when the Afghan War forced people to flee their homes. Taliban members were also Pashtun, the ethnic group to which most people in Kandahar belonged. The Taliban desired a government that would be based on a particularly strict understanding of Islam.

The Taliban's leader, Mohammad Omar (moh-HAHM-muhd OH-mar), had fought alongside the mujahideen

YESTERDAY'S HEADLINES

A New Era in Afghanistan

Several countries cheered when the Soviet-supported government fell in Afghanistan. The United States was among them. It meant the Soviets' power had successfully ended.

The United States and the Soviet Union had been in conflict for decades. Each side had desperately tried to limit the power of the other. The Soviets' loss in Afghanistan represented a larger loss against the United States. In fact, just before the Afghan government fell in 1992, the Soviet Union fell. Though conflict continued in Afghanistan, the United States felt that its support of the mujahideen had been a great success.

against the Soviets. After the Soviets left in the late 1980s, he had returned to Kandahar to start a religious school. He eventually earned the title of *mullah* (MUL-lah), or religious leader. As violence grew among mujahideen and rebel groups, Mullah Omar took action.

Some sources say that Mullah Omar claimed to have a holy vision that commanded him to restore peace. This inspired him to gather fellow students into the Taliban. He hoped to lead his followers into taking control of Afghanistan.

Muslims pray five times each day.

The Rise to Power

In 1994, the Taliban began its fight to take over. It quickly took control of Kandahar, its home region, and its power soon extended across southern Afghanistan. By this time, the group had gained support from other Afghans with similar religious beliefs as well as from other countries, especially Pakistan. The Taliban also benefited from training and weapons it had received from the United States and Pakistan during the mujahideen days.

By 1996, the Taliban had set its sights on Kabul. It quickly defeated the other rebel groups and the remaining mujahideen. Once the Taliban controlled Kabul, Mullah Omar established himself as head of the government. In 1997, Afghanistan became the Islamic Emirate of Afghanistan.

National Reform

The Taliban quickly forced its **extremist** Islamic views on the rest of the country. Women were required to stay out of the public eye at all times. Anytime they went outdoors, they had to wear cloaks called **burkas** that covered their entire bodies. They were not allowed to seek an education. Instead, they were forced to stay at home and serve their fathers or husbands.

The Taliban used severe punishment to control the population. Thieves caught stealing often had their hands cut off. Criminals were put to death for even small crimes. Non-Islamic religious objects were destroyed, including two ancient statues of Buddha.

The Taliban's treatment of terrorists brought a great deal of international attention. Terrorists use fear and violence to make political points. The Taliban allowed extremist Islamic terrorist groups to live and train in Afghanistan. One of the groups that arrived was called

Investigators from the United Nations study human rights in Afghanistan.

al-Qaeda (al-KY-duh
or al-KAI-duh).

A Deadly Decision

On September 11, 2001, al-Qaeda launched an attack on the United States. It flew two planes into the World Trade Center buildings in New York City. Another plane flew into the Pentagon, a major government building located near Washington, D.C. A fourth plane crashed in a Pennsylvania field after passengers attempted to stop terrorists who had hijacked the plane. Thousands of people died in the attacks.

SPOTLIGHT ON

Al-Qaeda

Al-Qaeda, which means "the base," was formed in the 1980s. Osama bin Laden originally created the organization to fight against the Soviets during the 1980s and 1990s. After the Soviets left Afghanistan, al-Qaeda continued to fight against governments it considered immoral, including the United States. Al-Qaeda has declared holy war against the United States more than once. The well-organized group has become known for its violent actions.

Following what became known as the 9/11 attacks, the United States contacted the Afghan government. They demanded that the Taliban turn over Osama bin Laden and other al-Qaeda leaders to the United States to be tried in an international court. The Afghan government refused to turn them in.

CHAPTER 2

OPERATION ENDURING FREEDOM BEGINS

British prime minister Tony Blair (left) was an important U.S. ally during the War in Afghanistan.

THE TERRORIST ATTACKS ON
September 11, 2001, shocked the world. Some
people were horrified. Others cheered. The people
of the United States wanted action. U.S. president
George W. Bush had been in office for less than a
year. He worked quickly to respond to the attacks.

The Central Intelligence Agency (CIA) and
the Federal Bureau of Investigation (FBI) quickly
determined that al-Qaeda was behind the attacks
and started collecting evidence against the group.
Meanwhile, President Bush asked other nations
for help. His plans for Afghanistan had two main
goals. The first was to take control of Afghanistan
away from the Taliban. The second was to destroy
al-Qaeda. Al-Qaeda leaders had to be found and
brought to justice, and the extreme practices of
the Taliban government had to end. The United
States would need international support to
accomplish these goals.

President Bush discussed plans with Prince Saud al-Faisal, Saudi Arabia's foreign minister, on September 20, 2001.

International Action

Within days of the attacks, several countries promised to support the United States. The North Atlantic Treaty Organization (NATO) did something it had not done in its 52 years of existence. This coalition of 19 countries declared that the attacks were attacks against NATO itself. The organization promised to provide any help the United States needed, including soldiers and money.

Australia and New Zealand offered portions of their armies, navies, and air forces. Even the president of Russia, formerly the Soviet Union, offered assistance. Japan sent three naval ships.

The United Kingdom was possibly the United States' greatest ally. From the beginning, UK prime minister Tony Blair gave his full support. UK troops were some of the first to enter Afghanistan.

The Battle Begins

On September 26, members of the CIA entered Afghanistan. They worked with anti-Taliban Afghan groups such as the Northern Alliance, a collection of tribal groups in northern Afghanistan. The groups had united to resist the Taliban in the 1990s. They had been fighting to prevent Taliban control in their region ever since.

The CIA helped organize the rebel groups. They gave the fighters weapons and other equipment. Special forces from the United States and the United Kingdom soon joined the fight.

A VIEW FROM ABROAD

After the attacks, governments around the world officially sent sympathy to the United States. However, individuals occasionally were not sympathetic. Posters, pamphlets, and calendars with images of bin Laden appeared in India, Pakistan, Indonesia, and a few other nations. Some of the people in these countries supported bin Laden and al-Qaeda. Others disagreed with the attacks. What everyone had in common was that they were all watching the United States to see what would happen.

Operation Enduring Freedom was in full swing by late 2001.

On October 7, Operation Enduring Freedom officially began. Planes bombed locations where Taliban or al-Qaeda members were believed to be. U.S. and UK troops fought their way toward the capital alongside Afghan rebels. Northern Alliance forces reached Kabul in November. By November 13, the Taliban had left without putting up a fight.

The fighting moved south to Kandahar City. The Taliban considered the Kandahar region its home. In less than a month, the entire region fell to Afghan and international forces. Some Taliban and al-Qaeda members fled across the border to Pakistan. Others hid in the nearby, cave-filled mountains of Tora Bora. Government agents believed Osama bin Laden was with them.

The international forces chased the Taliban and al-Qaeda into Tora Bora. They made their way toward a section of caves where bin Laden and other leaders were believed to be. With U.S. and UK troops nearby, Afghan forces led the attack on the caves, but the attack failed. Bin Laden and his associates escaped to Pakistan.

A Partial Victory

Even though bin Laden escaped, the United States still considered the conflict a victory. The Taliban no longer controlled the Afghan government. Afghanistan could be guided into a safer, more secure position as a nation. The country would no longer be a safe haven for terrorists. The chase for bin Laden and his followers would continue.

Meanwhile, a new government had to be created. The United Nations (UN) organized a council of Afghan political leaders. The UN did not include leaders of

The caves of Tora Bora provided plenty of hiding places for Osama bin Laden.

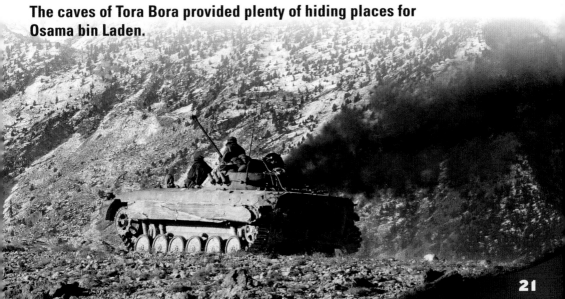

On December 5, 2001, the Bonn Agreement was outlined and agreed upon. A document was written to detail the agreement, including a description of the temporary government and the international military guidelines for the rebuilding of Afghanistan. See page 60 for a link to view the document online.

groups such as the Taliban in the council. In late November, as U.S., UK, and Afghan forces continued to fight against the remaining Taliban and al-Qaeda members, the council met in Bonn, Germany. On December 5, 2001, they agreed on a plan called the **Bonn Agreement**.

The Bonn Agreement was a blueprint for rebuilding Afghanistan. It called for international support and

The signing of the Bonn Agreement set the stage for Afghanistan's reconstruction.

22

guidance for a number of years to help Afghanistan grow into a self-supporting nation. In order to do that, the country needed a responsible government that its people would be willing to trust and follow. This would end rebellion in the country. A stable government would also make the country more financially stable.

In the meantime, an **interim** government would be created. A group of traditional Afghan tribal leaders was assembled to choose a chairman for the interim government. Among the nominees was Hamid Karzai, a member of the Afghan forces who had fought against the Taliban throughout the previous months. During the voting process, the United States openly supported Karzai. That support encouraged voters, and Karzai won the position.

TODAY'S PERSPECTIVE

Not Inviting the Taliban

The Taliban was still a threat after it fell from power. The people running the meeting in Bonn were afraid of violence and a return to old practices in Afghanistan if the Taliban got involved. As a result, Taliban leaders were not included in the Bonn meetings.

Since then, some people have argued that the Taliban should have been involved in rebuilding Afghanistan. Shutting it out of the Bonn council and the new Afghan government led to its continued fight for inclusion.

CHAPTER 3

REBUILDING

Afghan chairman Hamid Karzai (center) was a guest of President George W. Bush at his 2002 State of the Union address.

By THE END OF 2001, THE building blocks of post-Taliban Afghanistan were in place. Karzai was officially put in charge of the Afghan Interim Authority, with UN representative Lakhdar Brahimi as his adviser. New security forces were created, including the Afghan National Army and the Afghan National Police. Both would be trained by U.S. and other international forces. The new International Security Assistance Force (ISAF) arrived to help keep Kabul secure.

The UN promised $584 million to support the rebuilding process. Most of the money was intended for **humanitarian** aid such as water, food, safety, and education for the Afghan population. Some would also be used to end the conflict with the Taliban.

U.S. soldiers worked closely with the people of Afghanistan to rebuild.

A Relative Peace

In March 2002, foreign and Afghan forces defeated some 800 Taliban and al-Qaeda fighters. This was believed at the time to be the last major battle of Operation Enduring Freedom. The United States turned its attention to its invasion of Iraq.

Though pockets of **insurgency** remained, most people believed the conflict had ended. The Afghan population accepted the Afghan Interim Authority and the Bonn Agreement, and a variety of humanitarian projects were under way. Some 114,000 metric tons of food was delivered to Afghanistan. This was enough to feed six million people for two months.

The United States provided millions of dollars for the effort. Much of it went to rebuilding homes and other buildings. As much as possible was paid to Afghan workers in order to help Afghanistan's economy grow stronger by providing its population with income.

Bumps in the Road

Many people thought not enough was being spent on basic needs. The tons of food that had been delivered only fed a fraction of the 29 million people living in Afghanistan. Important long-term goals were being ignored. Schools and hospitals needed to be built, and so did homes and

YESTERDAY'S HEADLINES

End to the Conflict

In May 2003, U.S. secretary of defense Donald Rumsfeld made a speech announcing that major battles and fighting were over in Afghanistan. The country, he said, was moving into a rebuilding phase.

The statements seemed promising. Taliban fighting was limited. Such claims from Rumsfeld could encourage other countries to help rebuild Afghanistan. Weeks later, President Bush gave a speech supporting Rumsfeld's statements. Americans believed that the war was ending and hoped their troops might return home soon.

Foreign soldiers patrolled the streets of Afghan cities such as Kabul.

public buildings. Afghanistan needed water cleaning systems, and agricultural and industrial production needed to be improved.

More and more money went toward the growing military presence. By 2003, there were 8,000 U.S. troops and thousands more from other nations in Afghanistan. Attacks from the Taliban and other groups were still limited, but they showed signs of increasing.

Meanwhile, the ISAF was running into issues. The plan had been to have different countries take turns running the ISAF in six-month shifts, but the UN was running out of new volunteer countries. To solve the problem, NATO took over the ISAF in August 2003. Four months later, NATO decided to expand the ISAF's reach beyond Kabul. Over the next three years, the ISAF continued to expand its control. Afghanistan had been controlled mostly by U.S. troops, but by the end of 2006, most of the country was handed over to the ISAF.

A VIEW FROM ABROAD

In 2007, the British Broadcasting Corporation (BBC) polled Afghans on how they felt about ISAF and other foreign troops working in Afghanistan. According to the poll, 71 percent of the population supported the U.S. Operation Enduring Freedom, and about 67 percent supported the ISAF.

However, opinions varied widely from region to region. The relatively trouble-free north was happy. People in the south, especially the Taliban-filled southwest, were much more doubtful of the ISAF and U.S. missions.

A Permanent Government

The Bonn Agreement was intended to end after a few years with the establishment of a permanent government. The Afghan population would vote on a new president and members of **Parliament**. The UN and the Afghan Interim Authority planned to hold the elections in 2004.

Leading up to the elections, thousands of women were among the 100,000 voters to register. Some of the seats in Parliament were reserved for women. Several women ran for Parliament. One, Massouda Jalal, even ran for president, though she eventually withdrew.

During this time, threats of violence flooded in, and at least 1,000 people were killed. The attacks most likely came from the Taliban or Taliban supporters. Elections were delayed from their originally scheduled date in June. The presidential election was delayed first to September, then to October. Parliamentary elections were delayed into the next year.

Special training sessions helped Afghan women learn how to vote.

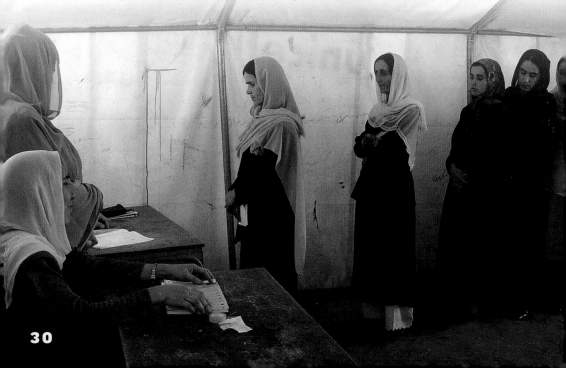

Thumbprints were meant to prevent people from voting multiple times, because the ink would stay on their hands as a sign that they had already voted.

UN and Afghan troops filled Afghanistan before and during the elections to provide security. Even with the threat of violence, the presidential election took place with relative success. Voters' thumbs were marked with ink to keep them from voting more than once. UN officials announced that 80 percent of registered voters had voted. Parliamentary elections finally took place in September 2005. Fewer voters turned out for these elections. Still, officials considered the elections a success.

A FIRSTHAND LOOK AT
PRESIDENTIAL ELECTION RESULTS

Voting results had to be approved by the Joint Electoral Management Body (JEMB). The JEMB included Afghan and UN officials who worked together to keep voting fair. In 2004, before Karzai was officially declared president, the JEMB signed a document approving the election results. See page 60 for a link to view the results online.

Election Results

Chairman Karzai became president with 55.4 percent of the vote. Several other candidates claimed there had been fraud. They believed several people had voted more than once. Some voting stations were also suspected

The other candidates were unhappy with Karzai's victory.

The 2004 election brought major progress for Afghan women.

of reporting false votes. Afghan and UN officials reviewed the voting ballots. They threw out hundreds of questionable ones. After this process, officials announced that Karzai had still earned the majority of votes.

In November 2005, the results of the parliamentary elections were announced. Women earned 28 percent of the positions in Afghanistan's new parliament. It was a major step toward equality for women.

CHAPTER 4

INSURGENCY

IEDs are capable of causing major damage.

EVEN THOUGH A NEW GOVERNMENT had been established, foreign troops still filled Afghanistan as 2006 began. NATO's ISAF forces increased from 10,000 troops to 20,000. U.S. Operation Enduring Freedom troops numbered around 20,000. Meanwhile, attacks from the Taliban and its supporters were becoming more common and more effective.

In January 2006, a suicide bomber killed a Canadian and at least two Afghans in Kandahar. The Taliban also introduced new weapons called **improvised explosive devices** (IEDs). IEDS are homemade bombs that are usually left near a road or building. The effectiveness of these bombs led to more success for the Taliban and its supporters. The insurgency against the new Afghan government and the foreign soldiers and volunteers steadily grew.

Red Cross workers attended a funeral service for their murdered coworker.

Humanitarian Issues

Attacks against foreign humanitarian workers had begun in 2003. One involved the shooting of a Red Cross worker. Horrified humanitarian organizations started pulling aid workers out of Afghanistan. The International Red Cross stopped activities in the area while it looked into its worker's death.

Violence built up steadily between 2003 and 2006. As troop numbers increased, the presence of aid workers decreased. In some places, aid workers disappeared completely. The UN ended humanitarian activities in the south of Afghanistan and slowed activities elsewhere. The U.S. Department of Defense determined that several areas were too dangerous for aid projects to continue. The limited funds that had been going to humanitarian aid were shifted to military support.

At the time, the Taliban generally used rocket attacks and raids. The rockets were often provided by foreign Islamic extremists who supported the Taliban's cause. Some of the rockets were part of the arms provided

Security in Kandahar was increased after the attacks on the Red Cross.

YESTERDAY'S HEADLINES

Red Cross Worker Executed

Ricardo Munguía was a water engineer with the Red Cross who was captured and shot by Taliban fighters in 2003. News of the shooting spread around the world. Articles described the chaos and violence in Afghanistan.

Some aid organizations asked for help from the international forces. They thought it would help if there were more troops in more places. Most nations, however, determined this would be too expensive and risky. Meanwhile, newspapers published stories predicting a sharp rise in violence.

years before in the fight against the Soviets. Raids were usually against aid workers or members of the new Afghan government.

The Threat Increases

The suicide bombing in Kandahar in 2006 marked a new **escalation** in the violence. The Taliban showed signs of better planning and support. IEDs became much more common. By August 2007, IEDs had caused a large number of the 240 deaths of U.S. troops.

The Taliban was funding its efforts through the opium trade. Opium is an illegal drug that is harvested from poppies. It is chemically turned into heroin, an expensive illegal drug sold around the world. Opium poppies have been grown

Poppy farms are a common sight in some parts of Afghanistan.

for centuries in Afghanistan. Under Taliban control, the opium trade had almost disappeared. Since being overthrown, the Taliban had found the poppy trade to be a fast and easy way to fund its fight.

In 2006, experts estimated that Afghanistan produced 90 percent of the world's opium. By 2007, this had grown to 93 percent, and it kept growing. The Taliban was paid to help transport the drug. It also was paid a tax by farmers growing opium in areas under Taliban control.

SPOTLIGHT ON

Improvised Explosive Devices

An old technology, IEDs have experienced new popularity in Afghanistan. IEDs are homemade bombs that are often made using explosives acquired from foreign militaries. They are buried, attached to cars, or left sitting on the ground.

The U.S. military has adapted to deal with IEDs. It has developed new ways to keep IEDs from exploding and also ways to explode them safely. However, as the military adapts, so do IED makers. The two sides consistently find new ways to outsmart each other.

Growing Support for the Taliban

More Afghans began to support the Taliban. Some supported its ideas. Others were encouraged by the increase in funds and effective violence. Some people supported it out of fear. Those who got in the way of the Taliban were often punished harshly.

One of the biggest reasons for growing Taliban support was the presence of U.S. and NATO forces. The Taliban was not a foreign outsider like the U.S. and NATO troops. Even more problematic was the way U.S. troops fought. The Taliban often lived in villages, among regular Afghan citizens. When U.S. or NATO troops fired on Taliban locations, other Afghans got in harm's way. Hundreds of citizens who had little or nothing to do with the Taliban were killed.

Many Afghan people were unhappy with the U.S. presence in their country.

Karzai's Problems

With the increase in violence, the Afghan government, which had initially gained acceptance, lost its appeal. Many Afghans accused the government of relying too much on foreign influence. Many believed that Karzai was weak and too involved with foreigners. Distrust of the U.S.-supported Karzai government led to support for the Taliban.

Afghan schools lacked many of the supplies their students needed.

Though women had seats in Parliament, they struggled to be heard. Women, especially in rural areas, still had little status. Furthermore, Parliament's and Karzai's promises to improve Afghanistan were not being fulfilled as planned. Schools and hospitals, once funded by international organizations, were not being built. Education and health care both suffered severely. The average lifetime of Afghan residents hovered around 45 years, about 30 years less than the average lifetime in the United States. Afghanistan's economy remained extremely poor. In a UN study, Afghanistan ranked 174th in development out of 178 countries.

A FIRSTHAND LOOK AT
A POLL OF THE
AFGHAN PEOPLE, 2009

In 2009, the Asia Foundation released the results of a poll of Afghan opinion. The poll covered topics ranging from the government to the opium trade and the Taliban. The report revealed a population with little faith in its government or the development projects in the country. See page 60 for a link to view the poll results online.

In addition, more of Afghanistan's population was facing Taliban intimidation. The organization was expanding its control north from Kandahar and Helmand. By 2007 and 2008, the Taliban had extended into about two-thirds of Afghanistan.

The Asia Foundation regularly polls Afghan people on their thoughts about the country's development.

CHAPTER 5

OBAMA'S NEW PLAN

Barack Obama's presidency brought about new plans for Afghanistan.

T‍HE INSURGENCY CONTINUED
into 2008. Meanwhile, the United States voted in
a new president. Barack Obama, a U.S. senator
from Illinois, began his presidency in 2009.
Within months, more U.S. troops were sent to
Afghanistan. President Obama also spent time
with his advisers, hoping to create a new, more
effective plan to help Afghanistan.

Afghanistan prepared for its own presidential
election. Many in Afghanistan and around the
world were nervous about the elections. The rising
strength of the Taliban and lack of faith in the
Afghan government did not bode well.

Obama worked closely with General McChrystal and other military leaders.

Peace and Safety

Throughout 2009, President Obama and his advisers worked to create a new plan. In February, the number of U.S. troops in Afghanistan was increased to around 50,000. In May, Obama placed General Stanley McChrystal in charge of Operation Enduring Freedom.

The plan focused on protecting the Afghan people. Fighting an insurgency requires winning the support of the population. A key aspect of winning support is keeping the population from harm, including harm from the Taliban. More importantly, it meant preventing Afghan citizens from being harmed by U.S. troops.

General McChrystal helped create a new method of fighting that could prevent innocent Afghans from being accidentally killed. The new method also emphasized handing power over to Afghan officials. This way, fewer U.S. troops would be needed in the future. U.S. and Afghan troops would work together to drive Taliban fighters from neighborhoods and villages. Once the areas were safe and rebuilt, the Afghan troops would take over and the U.S. troops could leave.

The plan also included a new strategy for peace. Effort was made to convince Taliban fighters to leave the Taliban. It was hoped that these fighters, and eventually their leaders, would join the Afghan government, ending the insurgency.

A FIRSTHAND LOOK AT
OBAMA'S SPEECH AT WEST POINT

On December 1, 2009, President Obama gave a speech at West Point, a U.S. military academy in New York. The speech detailed his plans in Afghanistan and Pakistan, and his vision for the future of Afghanistan. See page 60 for a link to watch a video of the speech online.

More Troops and More Problems

By the summer of 2010, 30,000 more U.S. troops were sent to Afghanistan. The operation was also widened to include Pakistan. Though Pakistan was not an enemy country, al-Qaeda and Taliban members were hiding there.

The plan resulted in some problems. More soldiers were injured or killed. Twice as many U.S. troops died in the first three months of 2010 than in the same time period of 2009. Furthermore, Afghan troops were not able to take over as quickly as was hoped.

As this went on, President Karzai made his own efforts toward peace. In 2008, he began meeting with Taliban officials. He even offered to meet with

The number of U.S. troops in Afghanistan was increased in 2010.

Taliban leader Mullah Omar. However, the talks largely came to nothing, and violence continued.

Presidential Elections of 2009

President Karzai's five-year term was coming to an end. So were the terms of members of Parliament. The UN helped Afghan officials organize the next elections.

The presidential election was scheduled for August 20, 2009. Around 30 people ran for president, including Karzai. As in the

A VIEW FROM ABROAD

Countries around Afghanistan offered to aid President Karzai in his meetings with the Taliban. Pakistan offered to organize the talks and make sure they were fair. But the United States feared that Pakistan was too supportive of the Taliban and so did not want Pakistan involved.

Karzai asked Saudi Arabia to help at one point. However, the United States and NATO both discouraged this. By 2010, it was determined that NATO would help with the peace talks. President Obama, meanwhile, encouraged Karzai to let Afghans run the talks.

previous election, threats of violence poured in. NATO troops were sent to protect voting stations. Even with the added protection, the violence was more serious than in the previous election. At least 26 people were killed. As before, voters inked their fingers to vote. After voting, some were attacked by Taliban fighters, and their inked

اوزبک، ترکمن، ایماق، تاجیک
شتون، هزاره، نورستان لیک
په ایی و باشقه نجیب و شرافت
ی ملیت لر، بیربیر لری بیلن
انئاه دیر لر.

Abdullah Abdullah was a popular presidential candidate in the 2009 election.

fingers were cut off. Several others were beaten severely before they had a chance to vote.

Millions of Afghans voted. Still, this was less than half of the people who had registered. In some parts of the south, less than 10 percent of registered voters actually voted. To make matters worse, several people claimed the election results were completely untrue. Karzai originally got 52 percent of the vote. Abdullah Abdullah, a medical doctor and former anti-Taliban fighter, came in second. When officials reviewed the votes, at least one-third of Karzai's votes were found to be fake. About 800 voting stations that had turned in votes had never actually opened. Many people voted more than once.

A **run-off election** between Karzai and Abdullah was scheduled for November. A month before the election was to take place, Abdullah withdrew. He claimed the run-off election would be as bad as the August 20 election. This left the title of president to Karzai.

The Continued Search for a Solution

The parliamentary elections on September 18, 2010, were no better. Candidates openly purchased votes. Hundreds of voters were killed, beaten, or threatened. Because of fraud and the problems with voting, Afghanistan was left with a weak government. The Taliban insurgency continued to fight against it, and the population continued to distrust it.

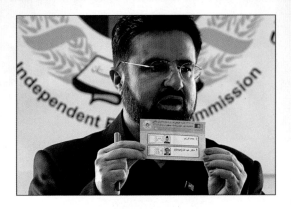

YESTERDAY'S HEADLINES

Presidential Elections

People around the world paid close attention to Afghanistan's 2009 elections. Stories of beatings and fake votes filled newspaper pages. Some papers had reporters on the scene. They sent in updates throughout the day, writing about what they had seen and heard. Television news reporters were also present to give updates. Most considered the activities around the elections to be a reflection of how things were going in Afghanistan.

What Happened Where?

UZBEKISTA

TURKMENISTAN

AFGHANISTAN

IRAN

Kandahar City The city of Kandahar has been called the spiritual home of the Taliban. It is the largest city in Kandahar Province, where most members of the Taliban come from.

Kandaha ●

KANDAH

Kandahar Province The Taliban originated in the region of Kandahar. It has been known for its support of the Taliban.

HELMAND

Helmand The region of Helmand is home to a large portion of the opium trade. The Taliban has a great deal of influence in this region.

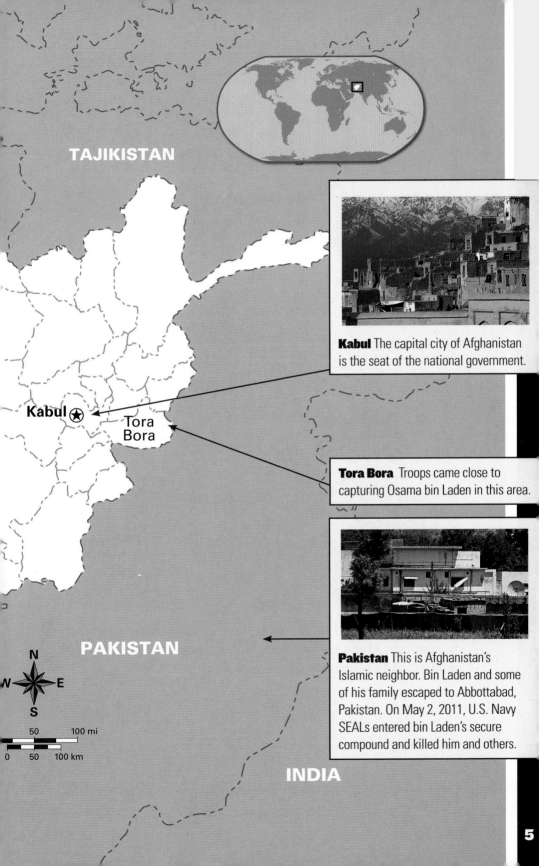

TAJIKISTAN

Kabul The capital city of Afghanistan is the seat of the national government.

Kabul ⊛

Tora Bora

Tora Bora Troops came close to capturing Osama bin Laden in this area.

PAKISTAN

N
W   E
S

50   100 mi

0   50   100 km

Pakistan This is Afghanistan's Islamic neighbor. Bin Laden and some of his family escaped to Abbottabad, Pakistan. On May 2, 2011, U.S. Navy SEALs entered bin Laden's secure compound and killed him and others.

INDIA

The Fight Goes On

A sergeant in the U.S. Marines plays with two Afghan children in southern Afghanistan. Many U.S. troops work directly with women and children in Afghanistan.

In 2011, the war in Afghanistan became the longest-lasting war in U.S. history. Plans early in the year

OVER 5 MILLION AFGHAN REFUGEES

predicted that U.S. troops would be present in Afghanistan at least until 2014.

Then, early on the morning of May 2, 2011, a team of U.S. Navy SEALs, helped by members of the CIA, raided a building in Abbottabad, Pakistan. Osama bin Laden and other members of al-Qaeda were believed to be inside. During a brief fight, bin Laden was found and killed.

News of the event was announced around the world. Messages from al-Qaeda promised revenge for their leader's death. Hours later, Taliban spokespeople sent a message warning that bin Laden's death would only encourage anti-American forces in Afghanistan.

Americans debated whether this was the end of the war in Afghanistan. Many in Congress argued that U.S. troops should leave Afghanistan as quickly as possible. Others argued that Afghanistan still needed help. The Taliban still refused to enter peace talks. Al-Qaeda members remained and many considered them still a threat. As of May 2011, U.S. and other foreign troops continued working in Afghanistan, training the Afghan army and helping Afghan citizens rebuild their communities.

George W. Bush

George W. Bush (1946–) was president of the United States between 2001 and 2009. He helped launch Operation Enduring Freedom after the terrorist attacks of September 11, 2001.

Osama bin Laden (1957–2011) was originally from Saudi Arabia but later became leader of the Afghan terrorist group al-Qaeda. In the 1990s and in 2001, he helped plan major international terrorist attacks. Early in the morning of May 2, 2011, U.S. Navy SEALs entered bin Laden's secure compound in Abbottabad, Pakistan, and killed him.

Hamid Karzai

Hamid Karzai (1957–) helped in the fight against the Taliban in 2001. He later became chairman of the Afghan Interim Authority and Afghanistan's first president after the fall of the Taliban.

Mullah Mohammad Omar

(ca. 1959–) fought as a member of the mujahideen against the Soviets. In the 1990s, he formed the Taliban and has led them ever since.

Barack Obama (1961–)

became president of the United States in 2009. He has radically changed the strategy in Afghanistan.

Barack Obama

TIMELINE

1996	2001	2003	2004

1996

The Taliban takes over Kabul.

2001

September 11
Al-Qaeda terrorists attack New York City and Washington, D.C.

October 7
Operation Enduring Freedom officially begins.

November 13
The Northern Alliance takes over Kabul.

December 5
The Bonn Agreement is created.

2003

August
NATO officially takes control of ISAF.

2004

October 9
Hamid Karzai is elected in Afghanistan's first presidential election, after the fall of the Taliban.

UN Talks on Afghanistan
Bonn, November / December 2001

2005 | **2009** | **2010** | **2011**

September 18
Afghanistan holds its first parliamentary elections, after the fall of the Taliban.

August 20
Karzai is elected to his second term as Afghanistan's president.

September 18
Afghanistan holds its second parliamentary elections.

May 2
U.S. Navy SEALs enter a secured compound in Abbottabad, Pakistan, killing Osama bin Laden.

LIVING HISTORY

Primary sources provide firsthand evidence about a topic. Witnesses to a historical event create primary sources. They include autobiographies, newspaper reports of the time, oral histories, photographs, and memoirs. A secondary source analyzes primary sources, and is one step or more removed from the event. Secondary sources include textbooks, encyclopedias, and commentaries.

Afghanistan Country Report on Human Rights Practices for 1998 This report is available through the U.S. State Department. It can be read online at *www.state.gov/www/global/human_rights/1998_hrp_report/afghanis.html*

Afghanistan Presidential Election Results — 2004 Hamid Karzai's 2004 election results are available through Afghanistan's Independent Electoral Commission. The JEMB document declaring him the winner can be seen online at *www.iec.org.af/public_html/Election%20Results%20Website/english/english.htm*

Afghanistan in 2009: A Survey of the Afghan People The Asia Foundation's 2009 poll of the Afghan people can be found on the foundation's Web site at *www.asiafoundation.org/country/afghanistan/2009-poll.php*

Bonn Agreement An online version of the Bonn Agreement can be found through the United Nations Web site. You can read the entire agreement at *www.un.org/News/dh/latest/afghan/afghan-agree.htm*

Remarks by the President in Address to the Nation on the Way Forward in Afghanistan and Pakistan President Barack Obama's speech about Afghanistan and Pakistan can be read or watched online. The White House provides a video and the speech's full text at *www.whitehouse.gov/the-press-office/remarks-president-address-nation-way-forward-afghanistan-and-pakistan*

RESOURCES

Books
Abrams, Dennis. *Hamid Karzai*. New York: Chelsea House, 2007.

Ali, Sharifah Enayat. *Afghanistan*. New York: Marshall Cavendish Benchmark, 2006.

Burgan, Michael. *Afghanistan*. Vero Beach, FL: Rourke Publishing, 2009.

Carlisle, Rodney P. *Afghanistan War*. New York: Chelsea House, 2010.

Gerber, Larry. *The Taliban in Afghanistan*. New York: Rosen Publishing, 2011.

O'Brien, Tony, and Mike Sullivan. *Afghan Dreams: Young Voices of Afghanistan*. New York: Bloomsbury Children's Books, 2008.

Price, Sean. *Osama bin Laden*. Chicago: Heinemann Library, 2010.

Willis, Terri. *Afghanistan*. New York: Children's Press, 2008.

Web Sites
Embassy of Afghanistan
www.embassyofafghanistan.org
Stay up-to-date with news from the Afghan Embassy in Washington, D.C.

Human Rights Watch: Afghanistan
www.hrw.org/asia/Afghanistan
Find out more about the social issues that affect Afghanistan's people today.

United Nations
www.un.org
Learn more about the activities and responsibilities of the United Nations.

GLOSSARY

Bonn Agreement (BAHN uh-GREE-mint) document describing how Afghanistan's government would be rebuilt after the U.S.-led invasion in 2001

burkas (BUHR-kaz) cloaks that cover the entire body and are worn by very traditional Muslim women

escalation (ess-kuh-LAY-shun) increase in speed or intensity

ethnic (ETH-nik) concerning a shared culture and history

extremist (ek-STREE-must) someone who holds radical views or promotes radical actions

humanitarian (hyoo-man-ih-TAIR-ee-un) that which improves the lives of other people

improvised explosive devices (IM-proh-vized eks-PLOH-siv dih-VISE-iz) homemade explosives

insurgency (in-SUR-jin-see) organized attempt to overthrow an established government

interim (IN-tur-im) temporary and transitional

mujahideen (moo-jah-hee-DEEN) Muslim religious fighters who fought against the government in Afghanistan

parliament (PAHR-luh-mint) a country's legislative body

run-off election (RUN-ahf eh-LEK-shun) a second election between two candidates who earned the two highest numbers of votes in the first election

INDEX

Page numbers in *italics* indicate illustrations.

ABOUT THE AUTHOR

Jennifer Zeiger graduated from DePaul University, where she studied English and religion. She now writes and edits children's books in Chicago. Many thanks to LCDR Michael Bates for his help with this project, and a few more to those who helped me find him.